Earning, Saving, Spending

Money

Margaret Hall

Heinemann Library
Chicago, Illinois

© 2001 Reed Educational & Professional Publishing
Published by Heinemann Library,
an imprint of Reed Educational & Professional Publishing,
Chicago, IL

Customer Service 888-454-2279

Visit our website at www.heinemannlibrary.com

Designed by Depke Design
Printed in Hong Kong

05 04 03 02 01
10 9 8 7 6 5 4 3 2 1

Library of Congress Cataloging-in-Publication Data
Hall, Margaret, 1947-
    Money / Margaret Hall.
        p. cm. - (Earning, saving, spending)
    Includes bibliographical references and index.
    Summary: An introduction to money, describing how it evolved to replace the
barter system, how it is used, different forms it takes, and currency in countries around
the world.
    ISBN 1-57572-233-X (lib. bdg.)   ISBN 1-58810-339-0 (pbk. bdg.)
    1. Money-Juvenile literature. 2. Money-United States-Juvenile literature. [1. money.] I Title.
HG231.H35 2000
332.4-dc21   99-046700

Acknowledgments
The author and publishers are grateful to the following for permission to reproduce copyright material: Cover photographs: Mike Brosilow (top), PhotoEdit/Michael Newman (bottom); International Stock/Scott Barrow, p. 24; Mike Brosilow, pp. 9, 11, 12, 13, 15, 16, 17, 19; The Picture Cube, Inc./Stephen R. Brown, p. 7; Rob Crandall, p. 18; PhotoEdit/Bonnie Kamin, p. 21; Culture and Fine Arts Archives/Eric Lessing, p. 6; The Picture Cube, Inc./Stephen G. Maka, p. 5 (left); PhotoEdit/Michael Newman, pp. 8, 22; North Wind Pictures, p. 4; Photodisc, pp. 10, 14, 15 (top), 20, 28, 29; Stock Boston/Robert Rathe, p. 23; Stock Boston/Eric Simmons, p. 5 (right); PhotoEdit/Dana White, p. 25.

Illustration p. 26-27, Tony Klassen.

Every effort has been made to contact copyright holders of any material reproduced in this book. Any omissions will be rectified in subsequent printings if notice is given to the publisher.

Some words are shown in **bold**, like this.
You can find out what they mean by looking in the glossary.

Contents

Before Money

A long time ago, there was no money. People didn't need any. They grew, gathered, or hunted their food. They built their own houses and made their own clothing. Sometimes people had things that others wanted. A woman who made beautiful pots might want a basket that another woman made. So they would **barter,** or trade, with each other.

American Indians traded with each other throughout North America, exchanging ideas and experiences as well as goods.

Sea shells were once used to pay for things.

Bartering worked most of the time. But sometimes people couldn't agree about what was fair. So they started to trade objects that had **value** to everyone. Salt, grains, feathers, tea leaves, shells, beads, and even fish hooks were used like money is today.

The First Money

As time passed, people traveled farther from home to trade. It was hard to carry things like salt, shells, and fish hooks. Someone came up with a better idea. Everyone agreed that metals like gold and silver were valuable. So people started to use them for trade. They made the metal into bars, lumps, or circles—the first coins.

Before using money, the Ancient Egyptians traded wheat and barley in exchange for metals, animals, spices, and lumber.

Like today's coins, some coins used long ago often had a picture of a **government** leader on them.

Before long, people all over the world used coins to trade for things. Many coins they used didn't look like the ones used today. But, like modern coins, they were easy to carry and had **value.**

Money Today

Today, most people don't **barter** for the things they need. They use money instead. Coins are still used, but they are only one kind of money. Another is paper money, or **bills.**

These children are using coins and bills to pay for their drinks.

The United States government changes the look of some bills to make it difficult for people to make illegal money.

The way money looks keeps changing. New coins and bills are made with different words and symbols on them. The materials used change, too. Instead of gold and silver, today's coins are made from combinations of more common metals, such as copper and nickel.

The Value of Money

Coins and **bills** are not worth much by themselves. The metals and paper used to make them do not cost much. So why do people think money is valuable?

This cash register is full of coins and paper money.

Money comes with a promise from the **government.** The promise is that every coin and bill is **legal tender.** That means that they can be used to pay for things. The government of the United States makes all the country's money. It is against the law for anyone else to make it. That is one reason why people trust the government's promise.

Coins

There are six coins used in the United States. Each one looks different and has a different **value**. How big a coin is does not tell you how much it is worth. Look at the dime. It is smaller than a penny or nickel, but it is worth more.

Dimes, quarters, half dollars, and dollars have ridges around their edges. The ridges help blind people tell which coins they have.

Susan B. Anthony was a famous American who worked to give women equal rights.

A Susan B. Anthony dollar coin is worth one dollar, but it is almost the same size as a quarter. People got the two coins mixed up, so the **government** stopped making the dollar coin. The Susan B. Anthony dollar coins were made only for two years, in 1979 and 1980. Many of them are stored away now.

Making Coins

Coins come from a **mint.** A mint is a factory for making coins. A coin starts out as a thin strip of metal. One machine acts like a cookie cutter. It cuts the metal into circles called blanks.

These pennies and nickels all started as blank circles.

The blanks travel to a machine that has special stamps called **dies.** The dies stamp symbols on both sides of the blanks. Coins are made very carefully. Every coin must look the same and weigh the same as other coins with that **value.**

Paper Money

There are different kinds of paper money, or **bills.** In the United States, they are all the same size, but each has different words and symbols printed on it. And each is worth a different amount of money.

Each bill shows the picture of a famous American.

A five dollar bill is equal to 500 pennies.

Paper money is handy. It doesn't weigh much or take up much space. So it is easier to carry than coins. A bill is usually worth more than a coin, too. If a book costs five dollars, it is easy to pay for it with a five-dollar bill. It would take 500 pennies to pay for the same book.

Making Paper Money

Paper money is made at the Bureau of Engraving and Printing, in Washington, D.C. Special paper and ink are used to make paper money. The paper starts out with nothing on it. Then it goes through a machine called a **printing press** that puts words and symbols on both sides.

Paper money is printed in large sheets and then cut to make each bill.

The serial number is under the *D* on this one-dollar bill.

Every one-dollar **bill** has the same words and symbols printed on it. But the bills are not exactly alike. Each one has its own special number, called a **serial number.** No other bill will have that number. The same thing is true for other kinds of bills.

Earning Money

People work to earn the money they need. The money they earn is their **income.** There are many ways to earn an income. People work in factories and restaurants. They deliver packages and mail. They take care of sick people and teach in schools.

People's incomes differ, depending on how much education, special skills, or training they have.

A paycheck can be taken to a bank and exchanged for money.

An **employer** pays a person money for the work he or she does. Many workers get a **paycheck** from their employers. You can earn money, too. Maybe you get paid for doing chores at home or in your neighborhood. The money you earn is *your* income.

How Money Is Used

People use the money they earn in many ways. People spend some of their **income** on **goods** and services. Goods are things people use, like clothing, houses — even toys. Services are things that are done for someone else. People pay doctors, teachers, waiters, and others for the services those workers provide.

Most people are careful not to spend all their money on goods and services.

The more money a person earns, the more taxes he or she must pay.

Most people save part of their income so they will have money in the future. And many people give some money away to help others. People must also pay **taxes.** The **government** uses tax money to pay government workers and to build things, such as roads and schools.

Making Choices About Money

There are many ways to spend money. Most people use much of their **incomes** to pay for their **needs.** These are things they must have. Food to eat, clothing to wear, and a place to live are all needs.

Everyone must buy food to eat.

Most people like to spend money to have fun.

People also spend money on **"wants."** Wants are things they would like to have, but could do without. Televisions, toys, and fancy cars are all wants. How to spend is not the only choice people make about money. They also decide how much to save and how much to give away. If they use their money wisely, they can do some of each.

Where Money Goes

When someone spends money, where does it go? Money travels from person to person and place to place. The five-dollar **bill** used to buy a book today might be in another town by next week. Just follow the travels of this bill.

1. A man gives a store clerk in Chicago, Illinois, a five-dollar bill to pay for a book.

2. The Clerk gives the same bill to a woman as change.

3. The woman puts the same bill in a birthday card for her nephew.

Money doesn't last forever. Coins get nicked or bent. Paper money gets dirty or ripped. But money isn't thrown away when it gets old. Banks trade worn-out coins and **bills** for new ones. The old money is sent back to the **government.** Coins are melted down at the **mint** and the metal is used again. Old bills are burned.

4. The mail carrier in Chicago picks up the card so it can be delivered.

5. The nephew in Dallas, Texas, takes the card from the mailbox.

6. He buys a toy and pays for it with the same five-dollar bill.

Money Around the World

The money used in other countries doesn't look like the money used in the United States. That is because every country makes its own money. The money of a country is called its **currency.**

Each currency is different. Coins and **bills** have different **values** and usually have different names, too. The symbols and words that appear on them are not the same either.

All of these bills are from different countries.

Visitors can change money at a bank or currency exchange.

If you visit another country, you usually have to use that country's currency. That doesn't mean that your money is worthless. It can be exchanged for the other country's currency. When it is time to go home, any money you have left can be changed back to United States currency.

Glossary

barter to trade one thing for another without using money

bill paper money

currency money used in a country

die tool used to stamp numbers and symbols on coins

employer person or business for whom other people work for pay

goods things people buy, such as food, clothing, and toys

government leadership of a country, state, or town

illegal against the law

income money a person receives from jobs and other sources

legal tender money that the government says can be used to pay for things

mint factory where coins are made

needs things a person must have in order to live, such as food, clothing, and a place to live

paycheck paper that is given to a person to pay for work he or she has done, that can then be exchanged for money

printing press machine that puts words and symbols on paper